Anger Management for Parents

EFT
Affirmations
Power Questions
Journaling

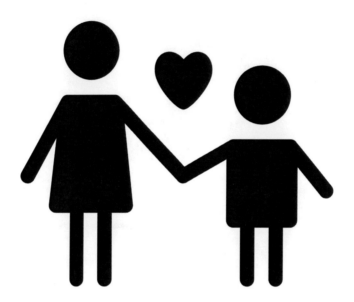

How This Book Can Help Change Your Life

It is hard to understand how a lovely baby can turn into a defiant toddler, or a rude anti-social teenager particularly when their siblings may be perfectly behaved. You can find yourself feeling constantly on edge waiting for the next drama to take place and then being easily triggered into shouting and intense anger which leaves you feeling ashamed and exhausted.

If it is any consolation most parents go through this! We wish we could be perfect saints and never lose our temper. but it seems like this child knows every button to push to trigger strong emotions which can lead to ongoing animosity and a simmering tension waiting for the next shouting match.

What can start to happen when your child has a forceful personality and lashes out because they want things their way, is that the temptation becomes to keep the peace and give in to their needs even if it is hurting your or other family members. Which can lead to a seesawing effect of overly permissive parenting where you just give in to keep the peace to outburst of intense anger when you come to the end of your tether and just explode.

This book provides simple effective and fast acting self-help techniques for parents with children of any age who find themselves out-of-control, angry and behaving in ways that are damaging to themselves and to their families.

The starting point to change is to realise that anger is always a sign that you have a belief, a set of values or standards that has been violated. Think about it... if you didn't have any expectations, you would never get angry with your child, they could do anything they liked and it would be ok.

The more expectations you have the more opportunities there are for conflict when those expectations aren't met. If you realise that it is always your standards of parenting that are at issue you can pick your battles and decide what is important in terms of bringing up your child. For example, you may let go of insisting they tidy their room if they are a teenager or you may avoid battles with siblings by buying two sets of the same toy, if they are young.

There are many amazing books that can give you strategies to deal with children and you can try and test lots of different strategies, but it all starts with identifying those areas of your family life that are essential and where your child is going to need some level of discipline.

When you decide what is important to you, what your boundaries are and what is in your child's best interest then you know there may be many battles ahead while you stand your ground and try to parent your child and steer them in the right direction.

This book is not about what to do to deal with an angry child, there are many other good books on that, this book is to help YOU...that's right YOU the parent reclaim your self-control and sense of inner peace while you deal more effectively and consistently with your child.

Additionally, maintaining control of your temper sets the example to that child of how to handle conflict and changes the dynamic in the household to a more peaceful atmosphere.

While you are trying to help the child move into understanding that you are a separate person with rights and boundaries and that there are certain things that are non-negotiable in terms of their behaviour you must protect yourself emotionally so you can respond more effectively because you feel calm and in control.

One of the best things you can do is start keeping a journal of your day-to-day interactions with your child to isolate what situations trigger them and you into conflict so you can put into place strategies to bypass the usual reaction.

I have included a journal at the end of the therapy exercises which you can use to pinpoint exactly what times, places, events, and thoughts are triggering your anger.

When you refer back to the journal and how you felt and reacted to events this is the perfect opportunity to use the EFT tapping protocols while you recreate these events in your mind and work through them systematically.

You can also write down new strategies to overcome issues and keep a detailed record of how they are working.

For example, a common trigger point with school age children is getting them out of the house on time to make it to school. Tempers can flare easily in these pressurised situations so it makes sense to put in place new practices that can bypass these trigger points, such as earlier bedtimes or stopping screen time after a certain time.

Keeping a detailed journal can help you identify these situations and then it makes it much easier to come up with new strategies or ways of behaving to stop the situation escalating into a shouting match.

The exercises in this book are drawn from my therapy practice with family members and are simple to understand and can be used for yourself and your child to help neutralise strong emotions and create paradigm shifts to help you view situations differently and respond more effectively.

These exercises are a combination of different types of therapy which can be used together to increase effectiveness.

1) Using affirmations to help reprogram your unconscious with the new way to respond to your child/children.
2) Using EFT tapping in conjunction with the affirmations or other positive statements to swiftly neutralise strong emotions and help create paradigm shifts which then causes you to respond differently.
3) Using Power Questions to contextualise situations and trigger creativity which makes it easy to come up with solutions and helps you to feel more empowered when dealing with family problems.
4) Journaling to help you recognise trigger points and put in place effective strategies to prevent things getting out of control.

How do Affirmations Work?

Affirmations are simple positive statements that work with repetition over time and have the impact of implanting powerful change messages into your unconscious mind. With daily application you should start to feel more peaceful and less easily triggered as your subconscious mind absorbs these positive instructions.

Say them throughout the day while you are doing other things such as going for a walk or doing housework, so they sink in easily to your unconscious.

- Choose the mixed affirmations and do ten repetitions for each affirmation OR choose a single affirmation and repeat it a hundred times at least twice a day OR choose a few affirmations and repeat each one a hundred times a day.

- Focus on those specific affirmations only, for thirty to sixty days until your emotional regulation has improved.

- Then move on to the next lot of affirmations if you feel you need it.

- Make affirmations a daily habit to keep you on the right track, think of them as daily exercises for your mind.

Affirmations to Transform Anger into Peace

- **I let go of self-pity, blame and anger and replace it with understanding and compassion**

- **I look on each angry outburst as an opportunity to learn and improve my parenting skills**

- **My peaceful state of existence is much stronger than any intermittent outburst of childish behaviour from others.**

- **Once an incident is over I learn from it and move on, I let go of past grievances**

- **If I do feel angry I remind myself that the problem is my response**

- **I set a good example with the way I handle strong emotions**

- **I am always looking for more effective ways to communicate to my family**

- **I release all expectations and deal with the here and now**

- **Everyday I do my best and that is enough**

- **I forgive myself for not being a perfect parent**

- **This episode will pass and be forgotten**

- **Anger arises due to my thoughts around the issue**

- **Anger is damaging to me and my family, I choose to replace it with calm acceptance**

- I put my boundaries in place and I stick to them regardless of emotional outbursts

- There is always a solution to a problem I am a problem solver

- I choose how to respond with my thoughts and behaviour

- I let go of thinking things aren't fair and deal with what is

- I release negative thought and behaviour patterns

- I release all resentment against my child and start each day anew

- I remain calm even when I am being provoked

- Managing my anger will strengthen my bond with my child

- I am proud of my ability to stay calm under stress

- I express myself in a calm clear positive way

- I am able to listen to other points of view and change when it is appropriate to do so

- Dealing with my anger is making my life better every day

- I am becoming more calm and centred every day

- I am in control of my actions I do not let strong emotions rule over me

- I take time to think before I react

- I choose to transform my anger into constructive actions that help to solve the problem

- Releasing anger only feels good in the moment then it is followed by regret

- I am calm and patient in the face of disobedience

- I am able to come up with solutions to every difficult situation

- I create reasonable rules and I stick to them

- I am not a bully and I will not be bullied by my child

- I love my child unconditionally

- I trust myself to be a good parent to my child

- It is important to say no when it is appropriate and stick to it

- Being a good parent is a worthwhile challenge

- Every day is a new day and a new opportunity for growth

- I can feel my anger and yet stay in control as it moves through my body

- I release the need to be right in favour of being wise

- I release the need to be in control of my child in favour of helping them to learn the lessons for themselves.

- I recognise that my child is an individual trying to express themselves.

- I recognise that their behaviour is not really directed at me and I don't take it personally

- I recognise that this behaviour is a result of some type of frustration and I am kind and understanding

- I am worthy of respect even if my child is disrespectful

- I am able to create boundaries and stick to them consistently

- I control my anger by changing my thoughts around this issue

- I recognise that my strong emotions are a sign that my thinking is flawed in some way

- I am able to create paradigm shifts that increase my ability to stay in control

- I can express my anger without shaming or frightening my child

- I replace anger with rules and actions that solve the problem

- I am always learning new techniques to deal with my child more effectively

- I take time to nurture myself in order to become a calmer more peaceful parent

- It is OK to say No and have boundaries

- I love my child unconditionally and show them that I love them every day

- I release what has happened in the past and let go of lingering resentment

- I'm becoming better at parenting every day

- Every day anger becomes less and less of a problem in my life

- I choose to respond calmly and rationally in all situations.

Power Questions to Increase the Efficacy of Tapping and Journaling

Often the problem of anger is related to some common beliefs we hold about standards and control that mean we become triggered easily. For example, if you have the belief that children should 'do as they are told' then when your child is disobedient you will be triggered to feeling angry.

Often feeling angry is a signal that we have and an unhelpful belief around this issue and if we can change the belief by examining it and replacing it with another more empowering belief then we should no longer be triggered as easily. Let me give you an example of what I mean.

I used to have the belief that my children should do as they were told, and I was constantly getting angry when they insisted on ignoring what I was saying and going their own way. However, when I replaced that belief with another belief that children were little independent beings who were trying to separate and assert themselves and that was a very natural and important process, I became more relaxed and allowed them to make their own mistakes so they could learn for themselves, which was much more powerful than me trying to tell them what to do. I only intervened when it was essential for their safety and as a result both my children have grown up extremely self-sufficient.

So, ask yourself these questions..

Is there a belief that I have that is making me angry when certain things happen?

What is that belief?

What would I have to believe instead in order not to be angry about this issue.

What processes could I put in place that would alleviate this problem?

Is there something that could be triggering this issue in my behaviour or in their external environment?

If so, what can I do to solve this problem?

It is very useful to have a special section in your journal to write down these power questions with solutions.

Here is an example of how to do this.

Your child refuses to go to bed and argues to stay up just a little bit more while they watch a tv program or play on the computer. This can go on throughout the evening and they can end up going to bed so late that they are tired in the morning and then refuse to get up which makes everyone late for school. Evenings turn into battles of will and huge shouting matches which leave you frazzled and exhausted and dreading the morning when the battle begins again to get your child up. You are at the end of your tether and don't know what to do.

Power Question One - How could I view this situation so I could stop getting stressed and angry?

1) My relationship with my child is more important to me than whether they go to bed on time.
2) This is just one of the problems of parenting it's perfectly normal and just a problem to be solved.
3) My child refusing to go to bed is not personal, they are not doing it to make my life difficult, they are just in the grip of something in that moment that we need to work out.
4) This is a problem we can work on together I have faith that we can work this out.

Power Question Two - What techniques could I put into place to help solve this problem.

1) I could look at this very analytically to see what is going on that makes my child not want to tear themselves away from the computer or TV. Are they becoming so absorbed they get 'stuck' inside the experience and find it hard to switch off.
2) I could see it not as the fault of the child but as the power of the computer or TV to hypnotise them so they can't tear themselves away.
3) I could see it as my child needs help to be able to transition from relaxing in front of the TV into a bedtime routine how could I implement a transitional period that they would enjoy.
4) It may be that the child has had a difficult day at school and is refusing to go to bed because they are dreading getting up. Is there something I can do to help them decompress from their day more effectively?
5) How about if I asked my child what I could do to help them to transition more effectively and let them come up with ideas.

You can see that this is a simple, yet powerful approach and it starts with the power question.

How could I view this situation so I could stop getting stressed and angry?

Here are some more powerful questions you can use to help shift from a reactive mode to a proactive mode where you are able to effectively handle the situation and cool down the emotional response.

When my child is grown how do I want them to remember me as a mother?

What example do I want to set to my children to help them become the best they can be?

What techniques can I use to cool my emotions when I start to feel angry?

How will I feel about myself if I am able to solve this problem?

How will the atmosphere in the household change if I am able to solve this problem?

Is blaming and shouting at my child an effective strategy for change?

What do other parents do to deal with this problem?

What are ten ways I could effectively test to see if they will solve this problem?

Are there any books or resources that deal specifically with this issue I could use?

Can I reorganise the household in a way that makes things easier for me and my child?

Sit down and think of questions that will trigger your amazing problem-solving ability and then refer back to them which you are feeling stuck. Try using them while you are doing EFT tapping as you will find your creativity can become unlocked using this process and you can come up with lots of amazing solutions direct from your subconscious.

EFT known as Emotional Freedom Technique also known as 'Tapping'

EFT stands for Emotional Freedom Technique also known as 'Tapping' and is a system of lightly tapping acupuncture points in the body while making statements about your emotions. This is an extremely easy fast and effective way of reducing painful emotions and creates paradigm shifts around the issue so you simply start thinking differently about the situation.

To make the affirmations and power questions much more powerful you can use them combined with EFT Tapping. You can download a chart of the tapping points at simpleselfhelp.net. or simply use the chart provided in this book.

Familiarize yourself with the points and then follow along with the sample tapping exercises until you feel confident that you can go off and do it yourself.

Tap the tapping points about 7 times lightly but firmly while you say the statements and focus on the feelings you are trying to change.

The point of EFT is to include statements of emotion and events that are personal to you so you simply replace the statements used in the examples with relevant statements that apply to you.

To measure how effective EFT is, take your emotional temperature around the issue on a scale of 1-10, think about it and try and raise your emotional temperature to as high as it will go, then start the tapping round and then take your emotional temperature again.

After a few rounds you should find that the emotional response is reduced, keep tapping until it is reduced to zero or one.

You will also find that you may have a different view of the situation or that you have some ideas of how to deal with it and have created a paradigm shift. You may also find that as one issue starts clearing other issues start coming to mind and you feel you want to move on to another issue. When that happens, write it down and make that the next problem to deal with after you have fully cleared the issue you are tapping on.

Tap Gently but Firmly About 7 times on Each Tapping Point Following the Sequence Below

Side of the Palm
The bony part
at the side of the hand

Top of Head
The middle part
at the top of the scalp

Above the Eye
The corner of the eybrow

Side of the Eye
The bony part
at the side of the eye

Under the Eye
The bony part
underneath the eye

Under the Nose
Just under the nose

Under the Mouth

Under the mouth above the chin

Under the Collarbone

The sore spot about 2 inches
underneath the collarbone

Underneath the Armpit

The sore spot a few inches
under the armpit

Finish off by tapping the side of the palm

EFT Tapping Chart

Here is an example tapping sequence which can be combined with affirmations or other similar positive statements that you tailor to you and your situation.

Repeat three times

Tap on the karate point 3 times while saying

Even though I feel really angry that my child has been rude and disobedient I choose to (replace with affirmation) release the need to be right in favor of dealing wisely with this situation.

Even though I feel really angry that my child has been rude and disobedient I choose to (replace with affirmation) release the need to be right in favor of dealing wisely with this situation.

Even though I feel really angry that my child has been rude and disobedient I choose to (replace with affirmation) release the need to be right in favor of dealing wisely with this situation.

Then start tapping on the tapping points and go round the upper body to complete a tapping round ending with tapping on the karate point to finish off.

Tap on top of the scalp while saying

I feel angry and disrespected but I choose to be calm and patient instead

Tap above the eyebrow while saying

My child is always being naughty and making me upset but I replace that anger with understanding and compassion

Tap at the side of the eye while saying

They are so unappreciative and selfish it makes me so angry however I choose to replace my feeling disrespected with understanding the situation and putting in place appropriate tactics to deal with the situation so it doesn't happen in the future.

Tap under the eye while saying

They are doing it on purpose to annoy me but I know that may mean they feel ignored and need attention so I will be understanding to that

Tap under the nose while saying

They infuriate me so much I feel like giving them a smack but I choose to restrain myself and practice the self-control I am trying to teach them instead.

Tap underneath the mouth while saying

I feel so annoyed that they have misbehaved this way I am fed up with all the drama I just want peace however I understand that this is something I just have to deal with

Tap the spot just under the collarbone while saying..

They have been so naughty that I don't think I can control my temper, but I choose to look for a solution to this issue instead.

Tap the sore spot about four inches underneath the armpit while saying.

It's difficult to calm down when I feel so disrespected, but I choose to remember they are a child not an adult and do not have the same level of self-control..

Come back to tapping on the karate point to finish off the tapping round.

I feel really angry that I have been so disrespected, but I choose to focus on the big picture which is being a good parent and responding appropriately to this situation when I am cool and calm.

Now take a few deep breaths and take your emotional temperature between one and ten. Is it still high? Keep doing more rounds until the emotion has reduced to between zero and one.

Over time anger can build up until it results in an ongoing feeling of resentment against your child which makes it easier to be triggered and harder to deal with the situation effectively.

Here is an example tapping sequence for releasing resentment which can be combined with affirmations or other similar positive statements that you tailor to you and your situation.

Tapping sequence to deal with a build of anger and resentment against your child.

Repeat three times..

Tap on the karate point 3 times while saying..

Even though I feel really resentful against my child I choose to release all feelings of anger and start again with love.

Even though I feel really resentful against my child I choose to release all feelings of anger and start again with love.

Even though I feel really resentful against my child I choose to release all feelings of anger and start again with love.

Then start tapping on the tapping points and go round the upper body to complete a tapping round ending with tapping on the karate point to finish off.

Tap on top of the scalp while saying..

I have let my anger build up but now I release it and start looking for the good in my child.

Tap above the eyebrow while saying..

I have been upset for a long time about their behavior but I now release all those pent up feelings and make a fresh start as a parent.

Tap at the side of the eye while saying..

Instead of noticing the bad things in my child I am going to focus on how much I love them and all the good things they do.

Tap under the eye while saying..

I have found it very difficult to let go of anger but I choose to replace anger with humor and patience

Tap under the nose while saying..

I have felt very angry about their behavior for a long time but that anger says more about my inability to effectively deal with the situation.

Tap underneath the mouth while saying..

I choose to replace this build-up of negative emotions with positive emotions of love calm and peace instead.

Tap the spot just under the collarbone while saying..

Instead of storing up resentment I look for effective ways to help my child fulfil their potential.

Tap the sore spot about four inches underneath the armpit while saying..

I choose to let go of all stored up feeling in favor of being the parent my child needs me to be.

Come back to tapping on the karate point to finish off the tapping round.

In the past I used to store up my anger but now I just let it go as soon as possible so I can return to feeling calm and peaceful.

Now take a few deep breaths and take your emotional temperature between one and ten. Is it still high? Keep doing more rounds until the emotion has reduced to between zero and one.

Using EFT with Power Questions when you need to come up with ways to solve problems.

Here is an example of how to use this method, let us say your teenage boy is very surly and refuses to clean his room.

Repeat three times.

Tap on the karate point 3 times while saying..

Even though I feel angry that my son won't clean his room I choose to come up with positive solutions instead.

Even though I feel really angry that my son won't clean his room I choose to come up with positive solutions instead.

Then start tapping on the tapping points and go round the upper body to complete a tapping round ending with tapping on the karate point to finish off.

Tap on top of the scalp while saying..

I feel very annoyed, but I choose to either come up with a positive solution or let it go.

Tap above the eyebrow while saying..

My son never brings down his dirty plates from his room what is a solution to this issue.

Tap at the side of the eye while saying..

He is so lazy it makes me mad but I'm sure there is a solution to this issue.

Tap under the eye while saying..

He needs to learn to keep his space clean and tidy like the rest of the house how do I motivate him to do that.

Tap under the nose while saying..

He infuriates me so much by not tidying up after himself, but I choose to see it as a problem that needs solving instead.

Tap underneath the mouth while saying..

I feel so annoyed that he behaves in this way but my nagging him is not working, if this issue is important to me I need to come up with a solution or else just not worry about it.

Tap the spot just under the collarbone while saying..

Sometimes it's hard to stay calm when I see his room, but I choose to look for a solution to this issue instead.

Tap the sore spot about four inches underneath the armpit while saying..

Although it makes me annoyed that he is so messy I need to remember that messiness is part of family life and I need to come up with strategies to deal with this problem.

Come back to tapping on the karate point to finish off the tapping round.

I feel really angry that my son ignores me when I ask him to tidy his room, but I choose to stay calm and focus on his good qualities while I come up with a solution to this issue.

Now take a few deep breaths and take your emotional temperature between one and ten. Is it still high? Keep doing more rounds until the emotion has reduced to between zero and one and keep a pen and paper handy as ideas and solutions for dealing with problems pop into your mind throughout the next few days.

Free Resources

Download your free PDF Chart of all the tapping points from **parents.simpleselfhelp.net** and sign up to get more EFT tapping sequences and get a FREE review copy of the audiobook version of this book which will have affirmations and eft tapping sequences to follow along with and makes the therapy even more effective.

parents.simpleselfhelp,net

How to Use the Journaling Pages

Situation Leadup: Record what was happening prior to the trigger event, was it something that just happened out of the blue? Was it the final straw in a chain of other events? How did you get to this point?

Trigger Event: What was the trigger event?

My Reaction: How did you react?

Power Questions: Create some power questions so you can come up with some great solutions to this issue, for example.

What processes can I put in place to make sure this never happens again?

What can I do to avoid being triggered by this situation?

How can I help my child, so they are able to behave more reasonably?

How can I show my child I love them while still showing that this is not acceptable?

Is there something in the environment that I am not aware of that may be creating this problem?

Is there something on my child's mind that makes them behave like this?

How can I work together with my child to solve this issue?

If you put your mind to it you can come up with some great questions that will inspire you to come up with powerful solutions to this problem so you can make sure that this is not a problem anymore.

EFT Tapping Sequence: Did you use EFT tapping on this issue what was the result?

Improvement Notes: Come back to this part after a period of time and assess what has changed and how things have improved.

Situation Leadup:
Trigger Event:
My Reaction:
Power Questions:
EFT Tapping Sequence Y/N Results:
Improvement Notes:

Journal

Situation Leadup:
Trigger Event:
My Reaction:
Power Questions:
EFT Tapping Sequence Y/N Results:
Improvement Notes:

Journal

Situation Leadup:
Trigger Event:
My Reaction:
Power Questions:
EFT Tapping Sequence Y/N Results:
Improvement Notes:

Journal

Situation Leadup:
Trigger Event:
My Reaction:
Power Questions:
EFT Tapping Sequence Y/N Results:
Improvement Notes:

Journal

Situation Leadup:
Trigger Event:
My Reaction:
Power Questions:
EFT Tapping Sequence Y/N Results:
Improvement Notes:

Journal

Situation Leadup:
Trigger Event:
My Reaction:
Power Questions:
EFT Tapping Sequence Y/N Results:
Improvement Notes:

Journal

Situation Leadup:
Trigger Event:
My Reaction:
Power Questions:
EFT Tapping Sequence Y/N Results:
Improvement Notes:

Journal

Situation Leadup:
Trigger Event:
My Reaction:
Power Questions:
EFT Tapping Sequence Y/N Results:
Improvement Notes:

Journal

Situation Leadup:
Trigger Event:
My Reaction:
Power Questions:
EFT Tapping Sequence Y/N Results:
Improvement Notes:

Journal

Situation Leadup:
Trigger Event:
My Reaction:
Power Questions:
EFT Tapping Sequence Y/N Results:
Improvement Notes:

Journal

Situation Leadup:
Trigger Event:
My Reaction:
Power Questions:
EFT Tapping Sequence Y/N Results:
Improvement Notes:

Journal

Situation Leadup:
Trigger Event:
My Reaction:
Power Questions:
EFT Tapping Sequence Y/N Results:
Improvement Notes:

Journal

Situation Leadup:
Trigger Event:
My Reaction:
Power Questions:
EFT Tapping Sequence Y/N Results:
Improvement Notes:

Journal

Situation Leadup:
Trigger Event:
My Reaction:
Power Questions:
EFT Tapping Sequence Y/N Results:
Improvement Notes:

Journal

Situation Leadup:
Trigger Event:
My Reaction:
Power Questions:
EFT Tapping Sequence Y/N Results:
Improvement Notes:

Journal

Situation Leadup:
Trigger Event:
My Reaction:
Power Questions:
EFT Tapping Sequence Y/N Results:
Improvement Notes:

Journal

Situation Leadup:
Trigger Event:
My Reaction:
Power Questions:
EFT Tapping Sequence Y/N Results:
Improvement Notes:

Journal

Situation Leadup:
Trigger Event:
My Reaction:
Power Questions:
EFT Tapping Sequence Y/N Results:
Improvement Notes:

Journal

Situation Leadup:
Trigger Event:
My Reaction:
Power Questions:
EFT Tapping Sequence Y/N Results:
Improvement Notes:

Journal

Situation Leadup:
Trigger Event:
My Reaction:
Power Questions:
EFT Tapping Sequence Y/N Results:
Improvement Notes:

Journal

Situation Leadup:
Trigger Event:
My Reaction:
Power Questions:
EFT Tapping Sequence Y/N Results:
Improvement Notes:

Journal

Situation Leadup:
Trigger Event:
My Reaction:
Power Questions:
EFT Tapping Sequence Y/N Results:
Improvement Notes:

Journal

Situation Leadup:
Trigger Event:
My Reaction:
Power Questions:
EFT Tapping Sequence Y/N Results:
Improvement Notes:

Journal

Situation Leadup:
Trigger Event:
My Reaction:
Power Questions:
EFT Tapping Sequence Y/N Results:
Improvement Notes:

Journal

Situation Leadup:
Trigger Event:
My Reaction:
Power Questions:
EFT Tapping Sequence Y/N Results:
Improvement Notes:

Journal

Situation Leadup:
Trigger Event:
My Reaction:
Power Questions:
EFT Tapping Sequence Y/N Results:
Improvement Notes:

Journal

Situation Leadup:
Trigger Event:
My Reaction:
Power Questions:
EFT Tapping Sequence Y/N Results:
Improvement Notes:

Journal

Situation Leadup:
Trigger Event:
My Reaction:
Power Questions:
EFT Tapping Sequence Y/N Results:
Improvement Notes:

Journal

Situation Leadup:
Trigger Event:
My Reaction:
Power Questions:
EFT Tapping Sequence Y/N Results:
Improvement Notes:

Journal

Situation Leadup:
Trigger Event:
My Reaction:
Power Questions:
EFT Tapping Sequence Y/N Results:
Improvement Notes:

Journal

Situation Leadup:
Trigger Event:
My Reaction:
Power Questions:
EFT Tapping Sequence Y/N Results:
Improvement Notes:

Journal

Situation Leadup:
Trigger Event:
My Reaction:
Power Questions:
EFT Tapping Sequence Y/N Results:
Improvement Notes:

Journal

Situation Leadup:
Trigger Event:
My Reaction:
Power Questions:
EFT Tapping Sequence Y/N Results:
Improvement Notes:

Journal

Situation Leadup:
Trigger Event:
My Reaction:
Power Questions:
EFT Tapping Sequence Y/N Results:
Improvement Notes:

Journal

Situation Leadup:
Trigger Event:
My Reaction:
Power Questions:
EFT Tapping Sequence Y/N Results:
Improvement Notes:

Journal

Situation Leadup:
Trigger Event:
My Reaction:
Power Questions:
EFT Tapping Sequence Y/N Results:
Improvement Notes:

Journal

Situation Leadup:
Trigger Event:
My Reaction:
Power Questions:
EFT Tapping Sequence Y/N Results:
Improvement Notes:

Journal

Situation Leadup:
Trigger Event:
My Reaction:
Power Questions:
EFT Tapping Sequence Y/N Results:
Improvement Notes:

Journal

Situation Leadup:
Trigger Event:
My Reaction:
Power Questions:
EFT Tapping Sequence Y/N Results:
Improvement Notes:

Journal

Situation Leadup:
Trigger Event:
My Reaction:
Power Questions:
EFT Tapping Sequence Y/N Results:
Improvement Notes:

Journal

Situation Leadup:
Trigger Event:
My Reaction:
Power Questions:
EFT Tapping Sequence Y/N Results:
Improvement Notes:

Journal

Situation Leadup:
Trigger Event:
My Reaction:
Power Questions:
EFT Tapping Sequence Y/N Results:
Improvement Notes:

Journal

Situation Leadup:
Trigger Event:
My Reaction:
Power Questions:
EFT Tapping Sequence Y/N Results:
Improvement Notes:

Journal

Situation Leadup:
Trigger Event:
My Reaction:
Power Questions:
EFT Tapping Sequence Y/N Results:
Improvement Notes:

Journal

Situation Leadup:
Trigger Event:
My Reaction:
Power Questions:
EFT Tapping Sequence Y/N Results:
Improvement Notes:

Journal

Situation Leadup:
Trigger Event:
My Reaction:
Power Questions:
EFT Tapping Sequence Y/N Results:
Improvement Notes:

Journal

Situation Leadup:
Trigger Event:
My Reaction:
Power Questions:
EFT Tapping Sequence Y/N Results:
Improvement Notes:

Journal

Situation Leadup:
Trigger Event:
My Reaction:
Power Questions:
EFT Tapping Sequence Y/N Results:
Improvement Notes:

Journal

Situation Leadup:
Trigger Event:
My Reaction:
Power Questions:
EFT Tapping Sequence Y/N Results:
Improvement Notes:

Journal

Situation Leadup:
Trigger Event:
My Reaction:
Power Questions:
EFT Tapping Sequence Y/N Results:
Improvement Notes:

Journal

Situation Leadup:
Trigger Event:
My Reaction:
Power Questions:
EFT Tapping Sequence Y/N Results:
Improvement Notes:

Journal

Situation Leadup:
Trigger Event:
My Reaction:
Power Questions:
EFT Tapping Sequence Y/N Results:
Improvement Notes:

Journal

Situation Leadup:
Trigger Event:
My Reaction:
Power Questions:
EFT Tapping Sequence Y/N Results:
Improvement Notes:

Journal

Situation Leadup:
Trigger Event:
My Reaction:
Power Questions:
EFT Tapping Sequence Y/N Results:
Improvement Notes:

Journal

Situation Leadup:
Trigger Event:
My Reaction:
Power Questions:
EFT Tapping Sequence Y/N Results:
Improvement Notes:

Journal

Situation Leadup:
Trigger Event:
My Reaction:
Power Questions:
EFT Tapping Sequence Y/N Results:
Improvement Notes:

Journal

Situation Leadup:
Trigger Event:
My Reaction:
Power Questions:
EFT Tapping Sequence Y/N Results:
Improvement Notes:

Journal

Situation Leadup:
Trigger Event:
My Reaction:
Power Questions:
EFT Tapping Sequence Y/N Results:
Improvement Notes:

Journal

Situation Leadup:
Trigger Event:
My Reaction:
Power Questions:
EFT Tapping Sequence Y/N Results:
Improvement Notes:

Journal

Situation Leadup:
Trigger Event:
My Reaction:
Power Questions:
EFT Tapping Sequence Y/N Results:
Improvement Notes:

Journal

Situation Leadup:
Trigger Event:
My Reaction:
Power Questions:
EFT Tapping Sequence Y/N Results:
Improvement Notes:

Journal

Situation Leadup:
Trigger Event:
My Reaction:
Power Questions:
EFT Tapping Sequence Y/N Results:
Improvement Notes:

Journal

Situation Leadup:
Trigger Event:
My Reaction:
Power Questions:
EFT Tapping Sequence Y/N Results:
Improvement Notes:

Journal

Situation Leadup:
Trigger Event:
My Reaction:
Power Questions:
EFT Tapping Sequence Y/N Results:
Improvement Notes:

Journal

Situation Leadup:
Trigger Event:
My Reaction:
Power Questions:
EFT Tapping Sequence Y/N Results:
Improvement Notes:

Journal

Situation Leadup:
Trigger Event:
My Reaction:
Power Questions:
EFT Tapping Sequence Y/N Results:
Improvement Notes:

Journal

Situation Leadup:
Trigger Event:
My Reaction:
Power Questions:
EFT Tapping Sequence Y/N Results:
Improvement Notes:

Journal

Situation Leadup:
Trigger Event:
My Reaction:
Power Questions:
EFT Tapping Sequence Y/N Results:
Improvement Notes:

Journal

Situation Leadup:
Trigger Event:
My Reaction:
Power Questions:
EFT Tapping Sequence Y/N Results:
Improvement Notes:

Journal

Situation Leadup:
Trigger Event:
My Reaction:
Power Questions:
EFT Tapping Sequence Y/N Results:
Improvement Notes:

Journal

Situation Leadup:
Trigger Event:
My Reaction:
Power Questions:
EFT Tapping Sequence Y/N Results:
Improvement Notes:

Journal

Situation Leadup:
Trigger Event:
My Reaction:
Power Questions:
EFT Tapping Sequence Y/N Results:
Improvement Notes:

Journal

Situation Leadup:
Trigger Event:
My Reaction:
Power Questions:
EFT Tapping Sequence Y/N Results:
Improvement Notes:

Journal

Situation Leadup:
Trigger Event:
My Reaction:
Power Questions:
EFT Tapping Sequence Y/N Results:
Improvement Notes:

Journal

Situation Leadup:
Trigger Event:
My Reaction:
Power Questions:
EFT Tapping Sequence Y/N Results:
Improvement Notes:

Journal

Situation Leadup:
Trigger Event:
My Reaction:
Power Questions:
EFT Tapping Sequence Y/N Results:
Improvement Notes:

Journal

Situation Leadup:
Trigger Event:
My Reaction:
Power Questions:
EFT Tapping Sequence Y/N Results:
Improvement Notes:

Journal

Situation Leadup:
Trigger Event:
My Reaction:
Power Questions:
EFT Tapping Sequence Y/N Results:
Improvement Notes:

Journal

Situation Leadup:
Trigger Event:
My Reaction:
Power Questions:
EFT Tapping Sequence Y/N Results:
Improvement Notes:

Journal

Situation Leadup:
Trigger Event:
My Reaction:
Power Questions:
EFT Tapping Sequence Y/N Results:
Improvement Notes:

Journal

Situation Leadup:
Trigger Event:
My Reaction:
Power Questions:
EFT Tapping Sequence Y/N Results:
Improvement Notes:

Journal

Situation Leadup:
Trigger Event:
My Reaction:
Power Questions:
EFT Tapping Sequence Y/N Results:
Improvement Notes:

Journal

Situation Leadup:
Trigger Event:
My Reaction:
Power Questions:
EFT Tapping Sequence Y/N Results:
Improvement Notes:

Journal

Situation Leadup:
Trigger Event:
My Reaction:
Power Questions:
EFT Tapping Sequence Y/N Results:
Improvement Notes:

Journal

Situation Leadup:
Trigger Event:
My Reaction:
Power Questions:
EFT Tapping Sequence Y/N Results:
Improvement Notes:

Journal

Situation Leadup:
Trigger Event:
My Reaction:
Power Questions:
EFT Tapping Sequence Y/N Results:
Improvement Notes:

Journal

Situation Leadup:
Trigger Event:
My Reaction:
Power Questions:
EFT Tapping Sequence Y/N Results:
Improvement Notes:

Journal

Situation Leadup:
Trigger Event:
My Reaction:
Power Questions:
EFT Tapping Sequence Y/N Results:
Improvement Notes:

Journal

Situation Leadup:
Trigger Event:
My Reaction:
Power Questions:
EFT Tapping Sequence Y/N Results:
Improvement Notes:

Journal

Situation Leadup:
Trigger Event:
My Reaction:
Power Questions:
EFT Tapping Sequence Y/N Results:
Improvement Notes:

Journal

Situation Leadup:
Trigger Event:
My Reaction:
Power Questions:
EFT Tapping Sequence Y/N Results:
Improvement Notes:

Journal

Situation Leadup:
Trigger Event:
My Reaction:
Power Questions:
EFT Tapping Sequence Y/N Results:
Improvement Notes:

Journal

Situation Leadup:
Trigger Event:
My Reaction:
Power Questions:
EFT Tapping Sequence Y/N Results:
Improvement Notes:

Journal

Situation Leadup:
Trigger Event:
My Reaction:
Power Questions:
EFT Tapping Sequence Y/N Results:
Improvement Notes:

Journal

Situation Leadup:
Trigger Event:
My Reaction:
Power Questions:
EFT Tapping Sequence Y/N Results:
Improvement Notes:

Journal

Situation Leadup:
Trigger Event:
My Reaction:
Power Questions:
EFT Tapping Sequence Y/N Results:
Improvement Notes:

Journal

Situation Leadup:
Trigger Event:
My Reaction:
Power Questions:
EFT Tapping Sequence Y/N Results:
Improvement Notes:

Journal

Situation Leadup:
Trigger Event:
My Reaction:
Power Questions:
EFT Tapping Sequence Y/N Results:
Improvement Notes:

Journal

Situation Leadup:
Trigger Event:
My Reaction:
Power Questions:
EFT Tapping Sequence Y/N Results:
Improvement Notes:

Journal

Situation Leadup:
Trigger Event:
My Reaction:
Power Questions:
EFT Tapping Sequence Y/N Results:
Improvement Notes:

Journal

Situation Leadup:
Trigger Event:
My Reaction:
Power Questions:
EFT Tapping Sequence Y/N Results:
Improvement Notes:

Journal

Situation Leadup:
Trigger Event:
My Reaction:
Power Questions:
EFT Tapping Sequence Y/N Results:
Improvement Notes:

Journal

Situation Leadup:
Trigger Event:
My Reaction:
Power Questions:
EFT Tapping Sequence Y/N Results:
Improvement Notes:

Journal

Situation Leadup:
Trigger Event:
My Reaction:
Power Questions:
EFT Tapping Sequence Y/N Results:
Improvement Notes:

Journal

Situation Leadup:
Trigger Event:
My Reaction:
Power Questions:
EFT Tapping Sequence Y/N Results:
Improvement Notes:

Journal

Situation Leadup:
Trigger Event:
My Reaction:
Power Questions:
EFT Tapping Sequence Y/N Results:
Improvement Notes:

Journal

Made in United States
North Haven, CT
08 June 2022

20018497R00074